CHART HITS
FOR BEGINNING PIANO SOLO

ISBN 978-1-70513-105-3

Visit Hal Leonard Online at
www.halleonard.com

Contact us:
Hal Leonard
7777 West Bluemound Road
Milwaukee, WI 53213
Email: info@halleonard.com

In Europe, contact:
Hal Leonard Europe Limited
42 Wigmore Street
Marylebone, London, W1U 2RN
Email: info@halleonardeurope.com

In Australia, contact:
Hal Leonard Australia Pty. Ltd.
4 Lentara Court
Cheltenham, Victoria, 3192 Australia
Email: info@halleonard.com.au

CONTENTS

4 ADORE YOU

8 BETTER DAYS

12 BLINDING LIGHTS

16 CARDIGAN

25 I HOPE

30 NEVER BREAK

36 SOMEONE YOU LOVED

20 TOO GOOD AT GOODBYES

40 WONDER

44 YOU SAY

ADORE YOU

Words and Music by HARRY STYLES,
THOMAS HULL, TYLER JOHNSON
and AMY ALLEN

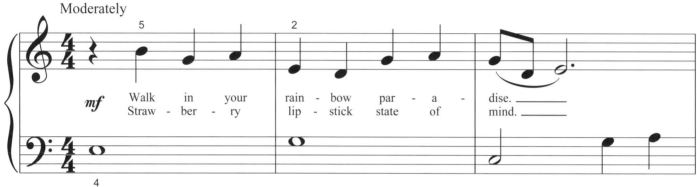

Walk in your rain - bow par - a - dise. ____
Straw - ber - ry lip - stick state of mind. ____

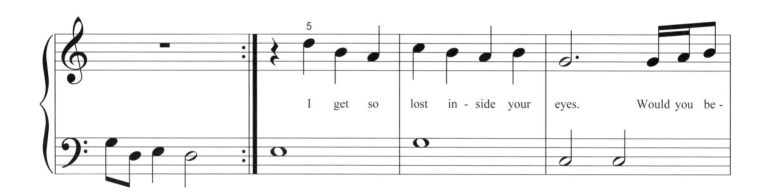

I get so lost in - side your eyes. Would you be -

lieve it?
You don't have to say you love me. You don't have to say noth - ing.
You don't have to say you love me. I just wan - na tell you some - thing.

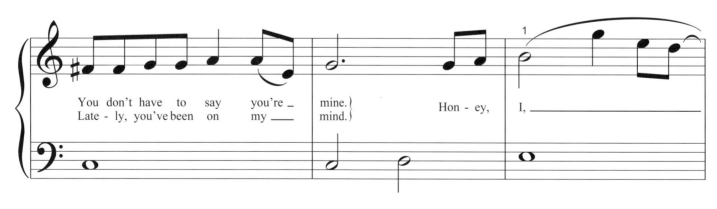

You don't have to say you're ___ mine.}
Late - ly, you've been on my ___ mind.}
Hon - ey, I, ____

5

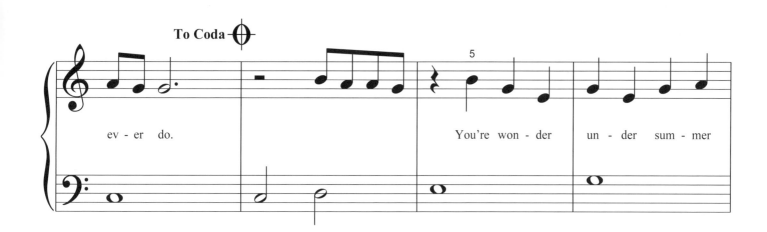

sky. _____

Brown skin and

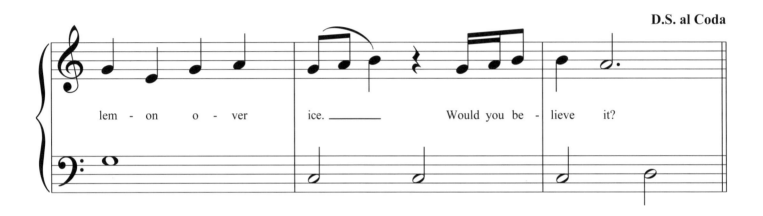

D.S. al Coda

lem - on o - ver

ice. _____

Would you be - lieve it?

CODA

It's the

on - ly thing I'll ev - er do. It's the

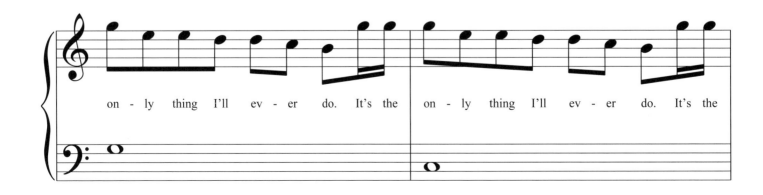

on - ly thing I'll ev - er do. It's the

on - ly thing I'll ev - er do. It's the

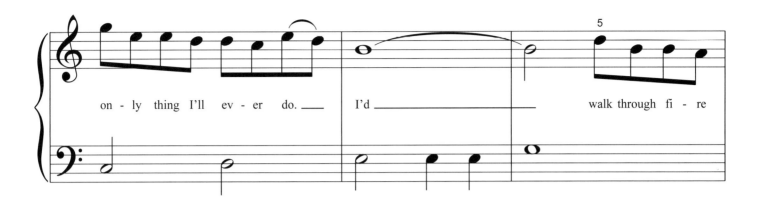

on - ly thing I'll ev - er do. ___ I'd ___ walk through fi - re

for you. Just let me a - dore you. Oh, hon - ey, I, ___

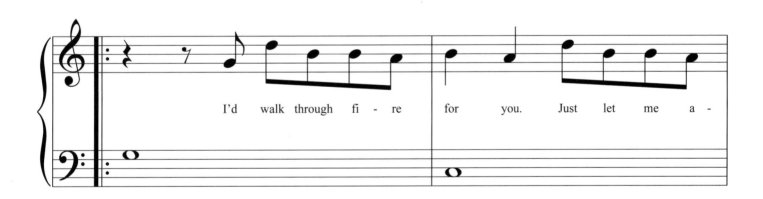

I'd walk through fi - re for you. Just let me a -

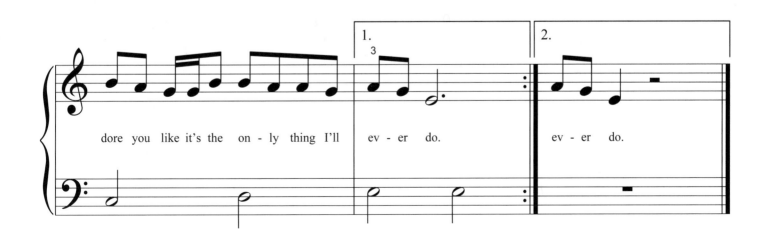

dore you like it's the on - ly thing I'll ev - er do.   ev - er do.

BETTER DAYS

Words and Music by RYAN TEDDER,
BRENT KUTZLE and JOHN NATHANIEL

Oh, I know that there'll be bet - ter days. __ Oh, that sun - shine 'bout to

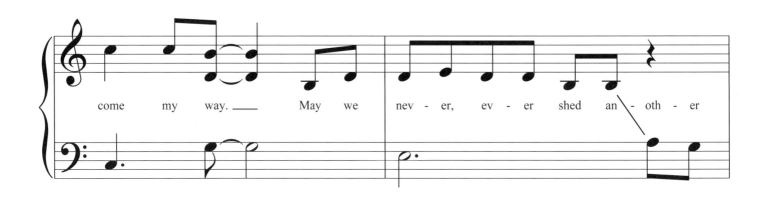

come my way. __ May we nev - er, ev - er shed an - oth - er

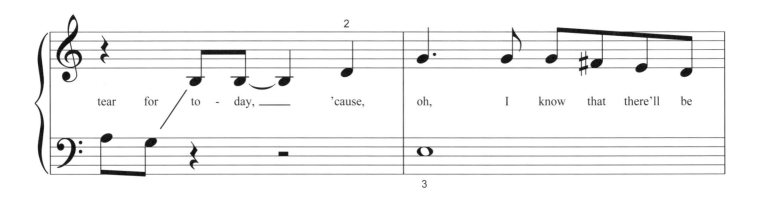

tear for to - day, __ 'cause, oh, I know that there'll be

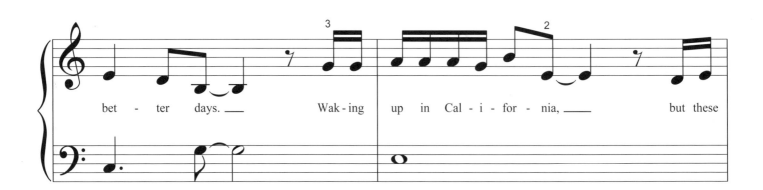

bet - ter days. __ Wak - ing up in Cal - i - for - nia, __ but these

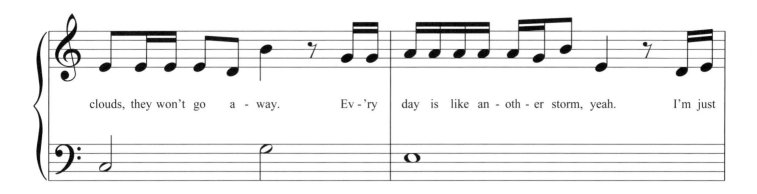

clouds, they won't go a - way. Ev - 'ry day is like an - oth - er storm, yeah. I'm just

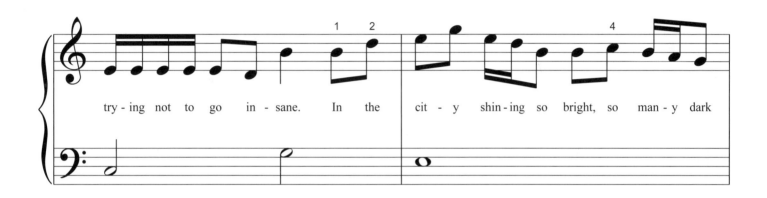

try - ing not to go in - sane. In the cit - y shin - ing so bright, so man - y dark

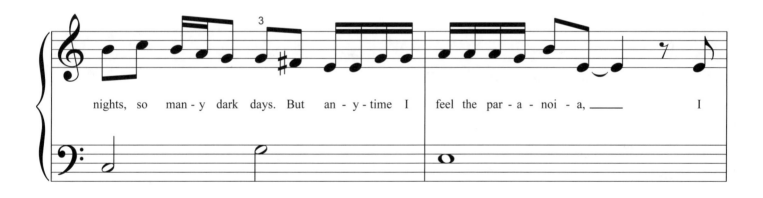

nights, so man - y dark days. But an - y - time I feel the par - a - noi - a, _____ I

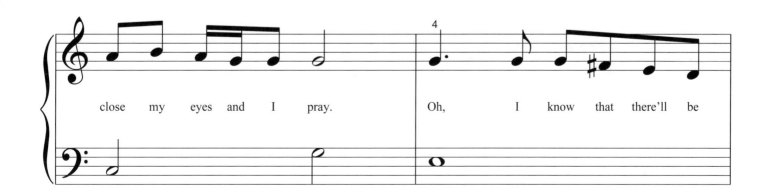

close my eyes and I pray. Oh, I know that there'll be

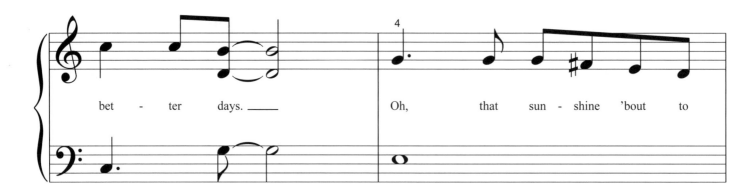

bet - ter days. _____ Oh, that sun - shine 'bout to

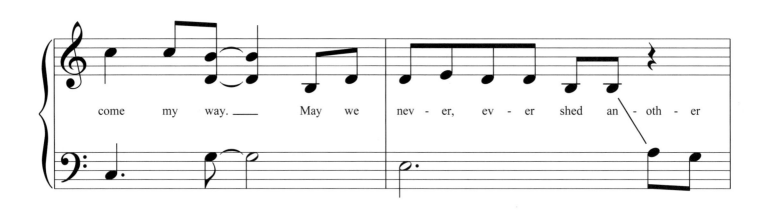

come my way. _____ May we nev - er, ev - er shed an - oth - er

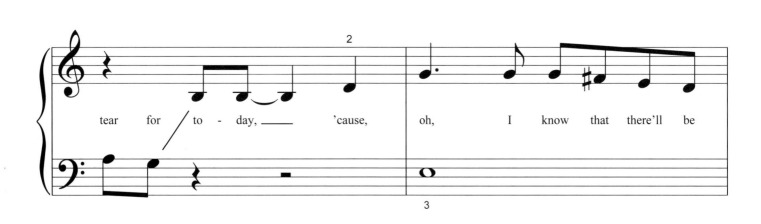

tear for to - day, _____ 'cause, oh, I know that there'll be

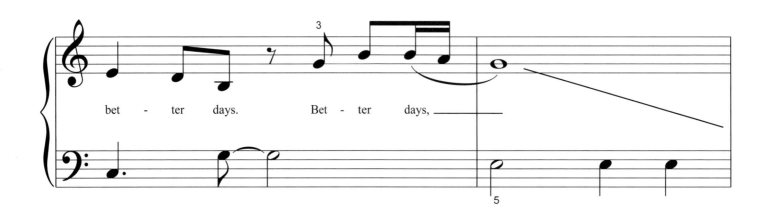

bet - ter days. Bet - ter days, _____

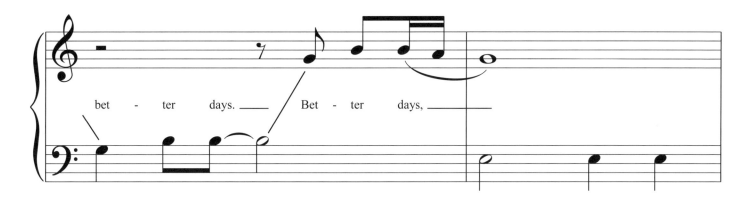

bet - ter days. _____ Bet - ter days, _____

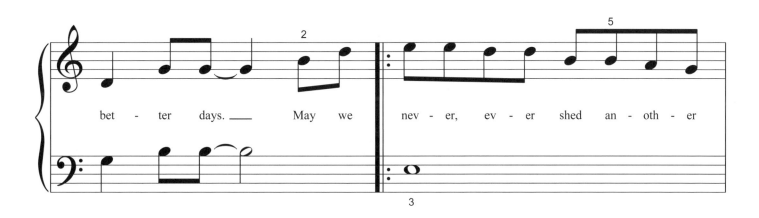

bet - ter days. _____ May we nev - er, ev - er shed an - oth - er

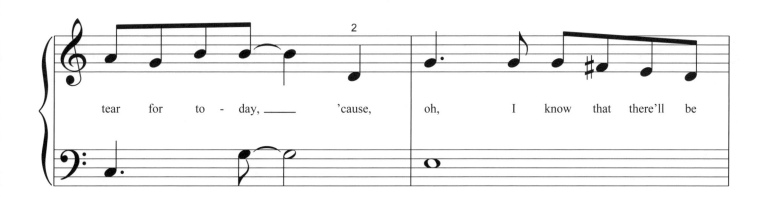

tear for to - day, _____ 'cause, oh, I know that there'll be

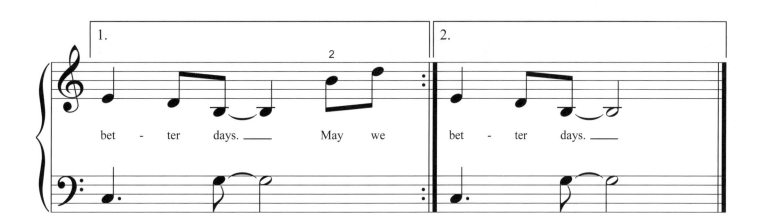

1.
bet - ter days. _____ May we

2.
bet - ter days. _____

BLINDING LIGHTS

Words and Music by ABEL TESFAYE,
MAX MARTIN, JASON QUENNEVILLE,
OSCAR HOLTER and AHMAD BALSHE

Fast dance beat

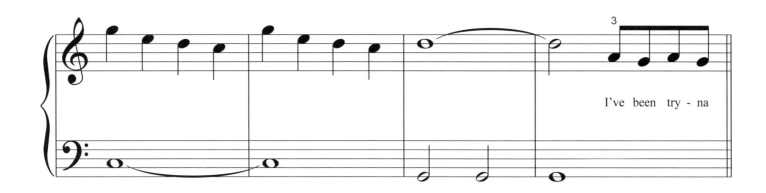

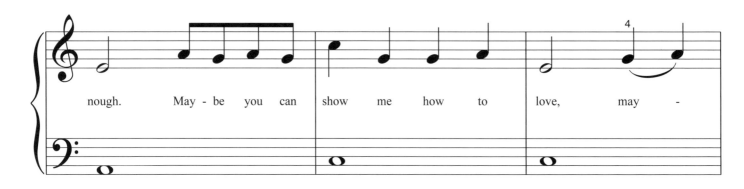

be. I'm go - in' through with - drawals.

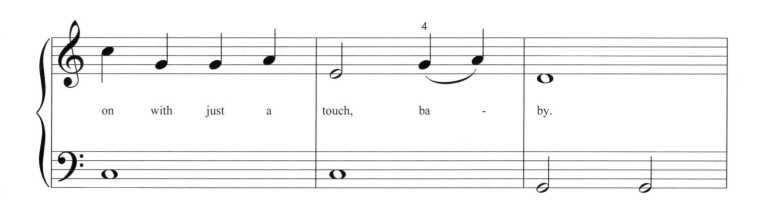

You don't e - ven have to do too much. You can turn me

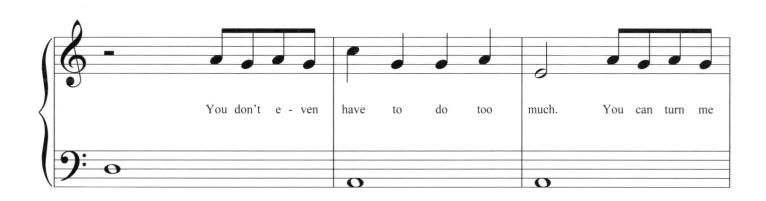

on with just a touch, ba - by.

I look a - round, but Sin Cit - y's cold and emp - ty.

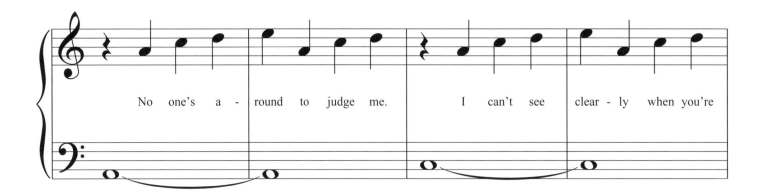

No one's a - round to judge me. I can't see clear - ly when you're

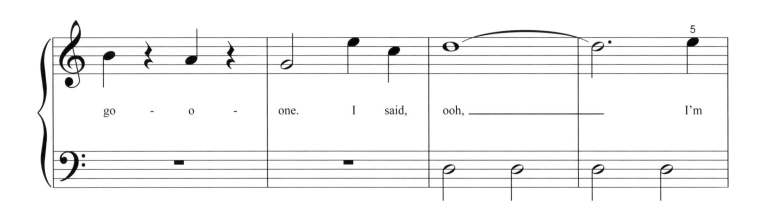

go - o - one. I said, ooh, I'm

blind - ed by the lights. No, I can't sleep un - til I feel your

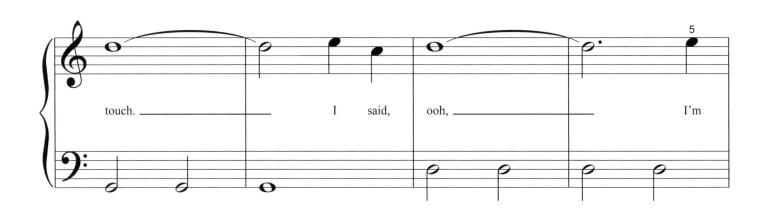

touch. I said, ooh, I'm

drown - ing in the night. Oh, when I'm like this,

you're the one I trust.

CARDIGAN

Words and Music by TAYLOR SWIFT
and AARON DESSNER

Slowly

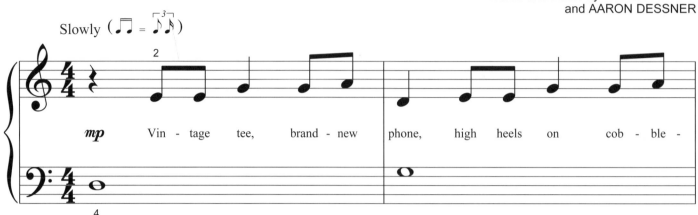

Vin - tage tee, brand - new phone, high heels on cob - ble -

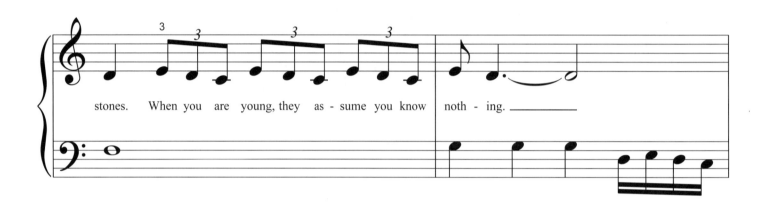

stones. When you are young, they as - sume you know noth - ing. _____

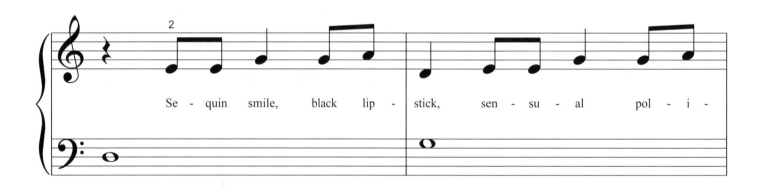

Se - quin smile, black lip - stick, sen - su - al pol - i -

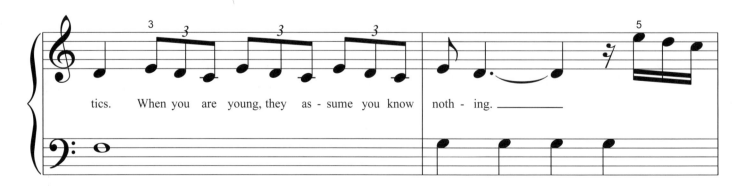

tics. When you are young, they as - sume you know noth - ing. _____

But I knew you, danc-ing in your Le-vi's, drunk un-der a street-light. I, _____

I knew you, hand un-der my sweat-shirt, ba-by, kiss it bet-ter. I.... _____

And when I felt like I was an old car-di-gan un-der some-one's bed, ____

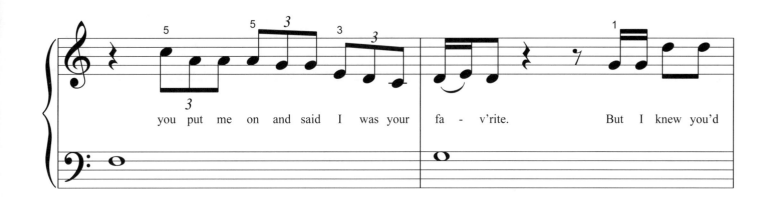

you put me on and said I was your fa-v'rite. But I knew you'd

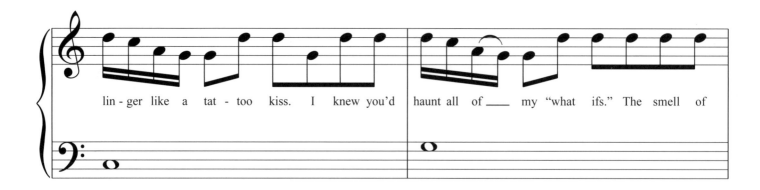

lin - ger like a tat - too kiss. I knew you'd haunt all of ___ my "what ifs." The smell of

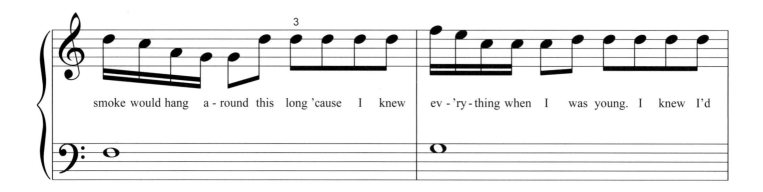

smoke would hang a - round this long 'cause I knew ev - 'ry - thing when I was young. I knew I'd

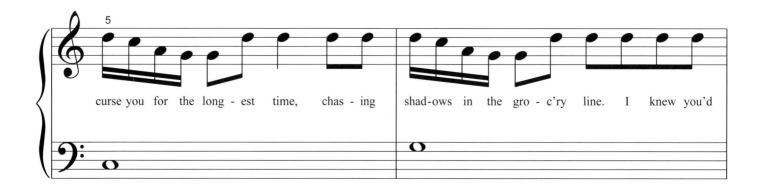

curse you for the long - est time, chas - ing shad - ows in the gro - c'ry line. I knew you'd

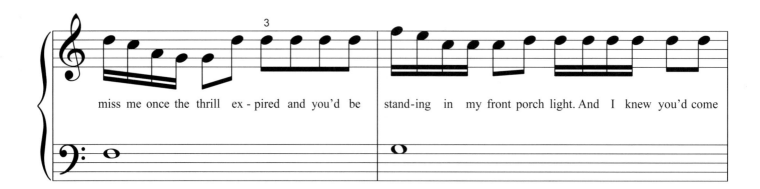

miss me once the thrill ex - pired and you'd be stand - ing in my front porch light. And I knew you'd come

back to me,   you'd come back to me.   And you'd come

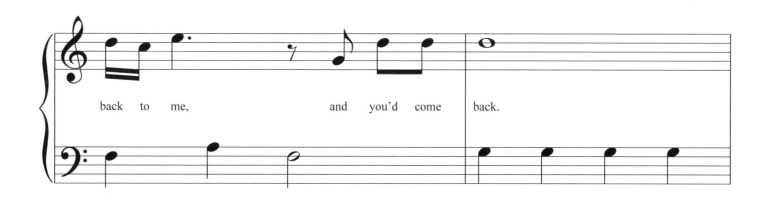

back to me,   and you'd come back.

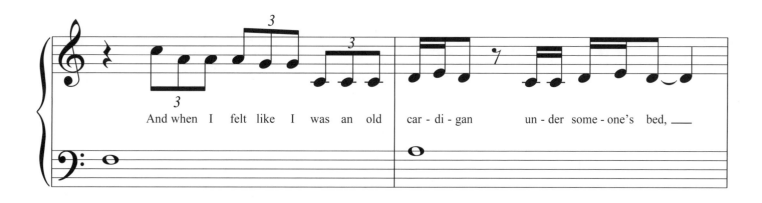

And when I felt like I was an old car - di - gan un - der some - one's bed, ___

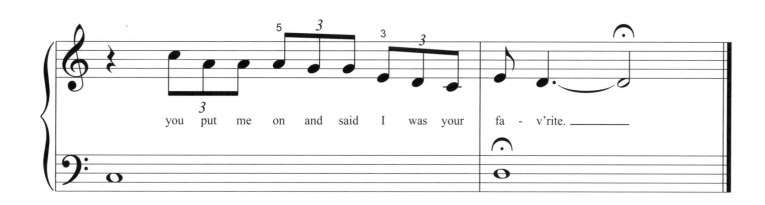

you put me on and said I was your fa - v'rite. _____

TOO GOOD AT GOODBYES

Words and Music by SAM SMITH, TOR HERMANSEN,
MIKKEL ERIKSEN and JAMES NAPIER

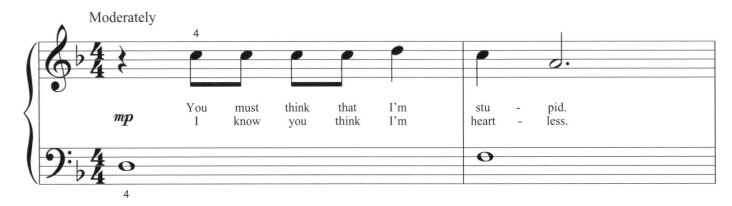

You must think that I'm stu - pid.
I know you think I'm heart - less.

You must think that I'm a fool.
I know you think I am cold.

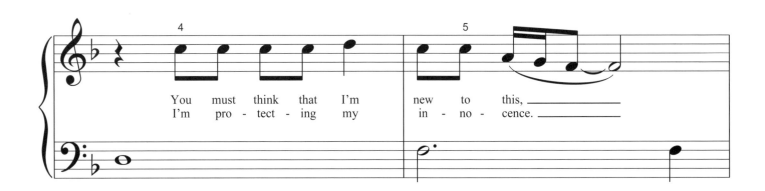

You must think that I'm new to this,
I'm pro - tect - ing my in - no - cence.

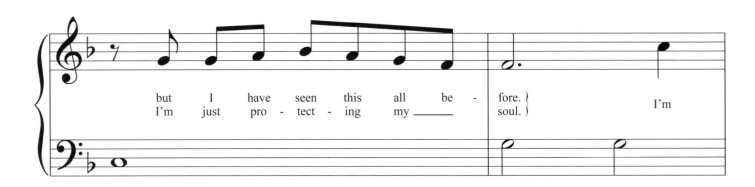

but I have seen this all be - fore.
I'm just pro - tect - ing my ___ soul.

I'm

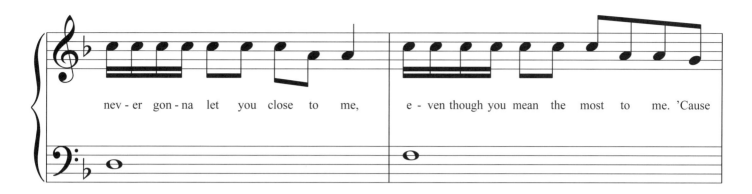

nev - er gon - na let you close to me, e - ven though you mean the most to me. 'Cause

ev - 'ry time I o - pen up, it hurts. _____ So I'm

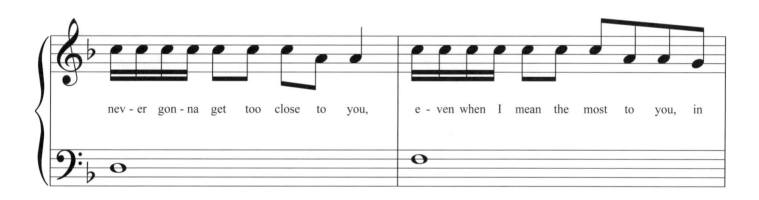

nev - er gon - na get too close to you, e - ven when I mean the most to you, in

case you go and leave me in the dirt. But ev - 'ry time you

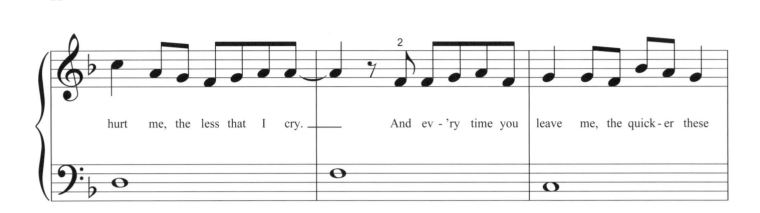

hurt me, the less that I cry. _____ And ev-'ry time you leave me, the quick-er these

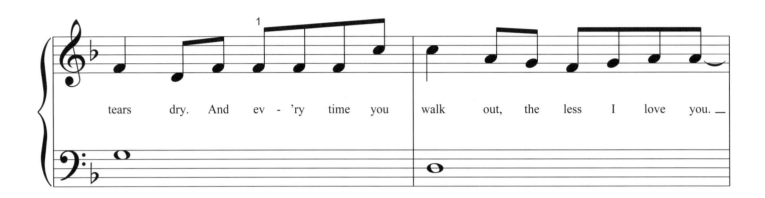

tears dry. And ev-'ry time you walk out, the less I love you. __

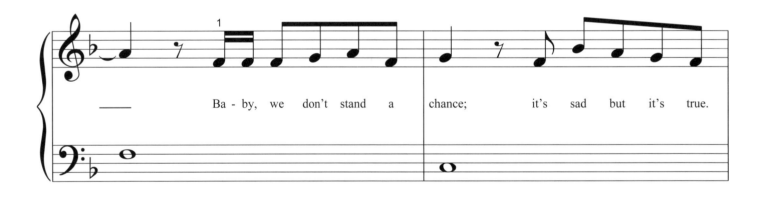

_____ Ba-by, we don't stand a chance; it's sad but it's true.

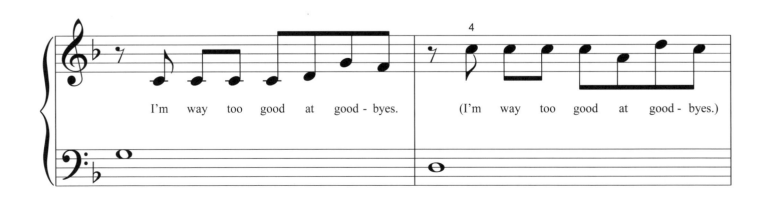

I'm way too good at good-byes. (I'm way too good at good-byes.)

I'm way too good at good-byes. (I'm way too good at good-byes.)

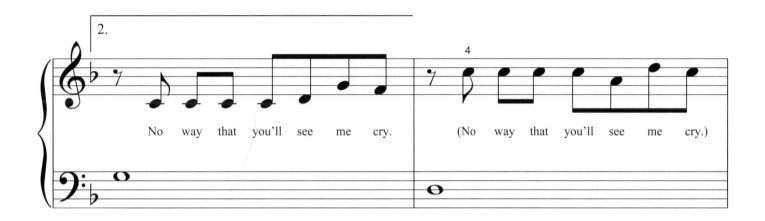

No way that you'll see me cry. (No way that you'll see me cry.)

I'm way too good at good - byes. (I'm way too good at good - byes.)

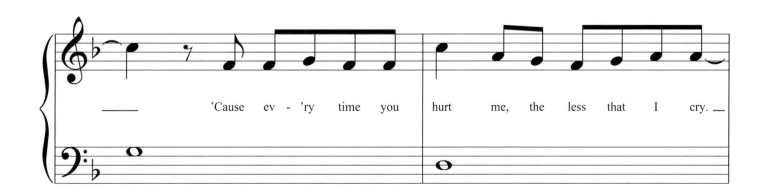

_____ 'Cause ev - 'ry time you hurt me, the less that I cry. _

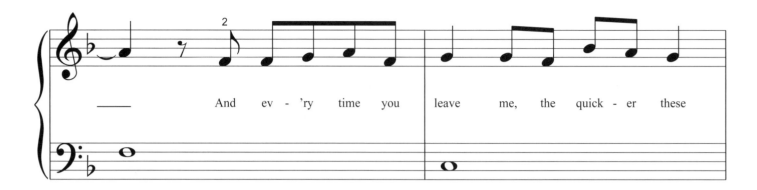

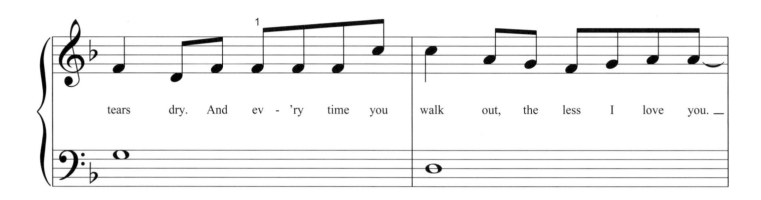

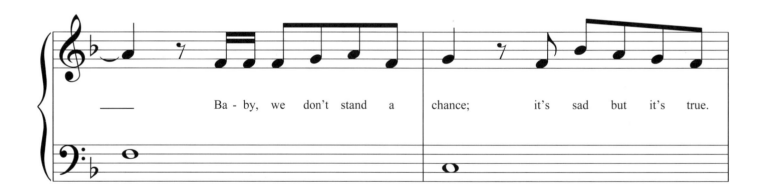

I HOPE

Words and Music by GABBY BARRETT,
ZACHARY KALE and JOHN NITE

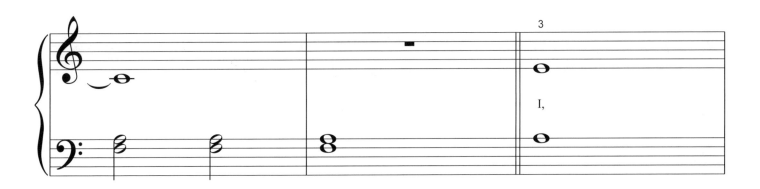

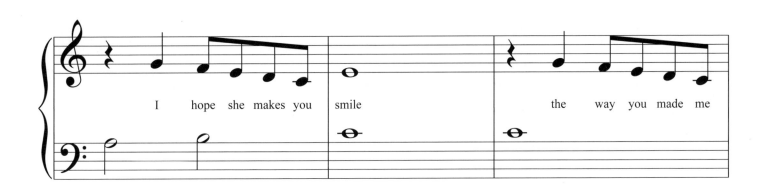

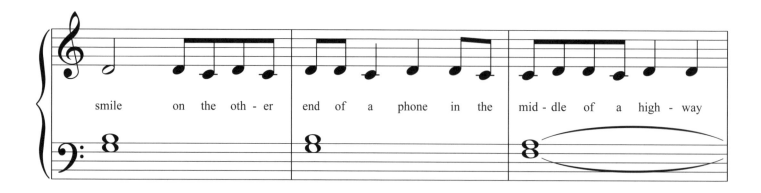

smile on the oth - er end of a phone in the mid - dle of a high - way

driv - in' a - lone. Oh, I, I hope you hear a

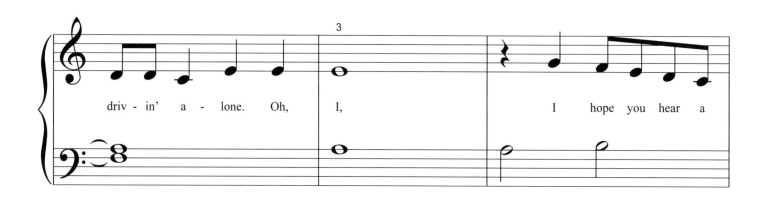

song that makes you sing a - long and gets you

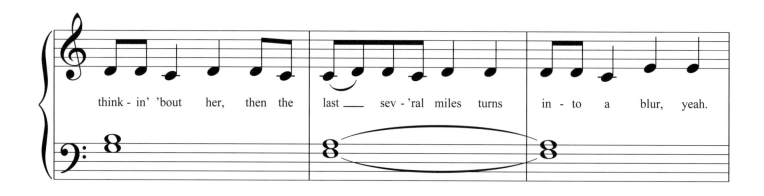

think - in' 'bout her, then the last ___ sev - 'ral miles turns in - to a blur, yeah.

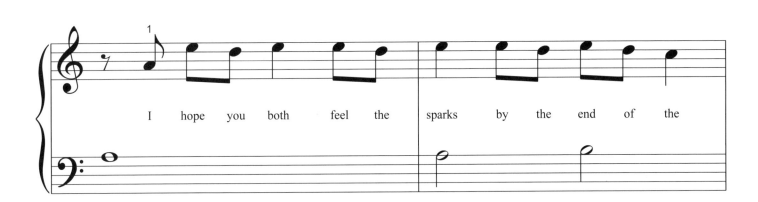

I hope you both feel the sparks by the end of the

drive. I hope you know she's the one by the end of the

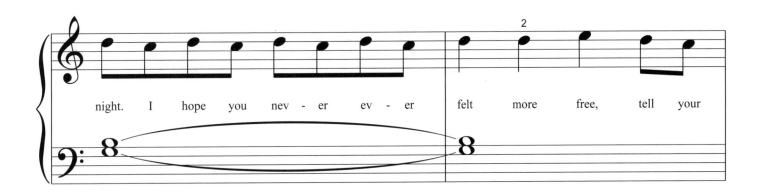

night. I hope you nev - er ev - er felt more free, tell your

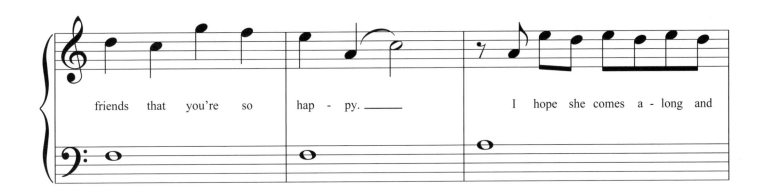

friends that you're so hap - py. _____ I hope she comes a - long and

wrecks ev - 'ry one of your plans. I hope you spend your last

dime to put a rock on her hand. I hope she's wild - er than your

wild - est dreams, she's ev - 'ry - thing you're ev - er gon - na

need. And then I hope she cheats like you did on

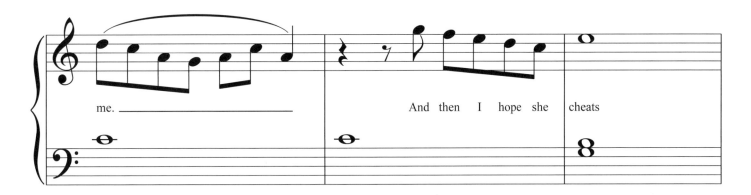

me. _____

And then I hope she cheats

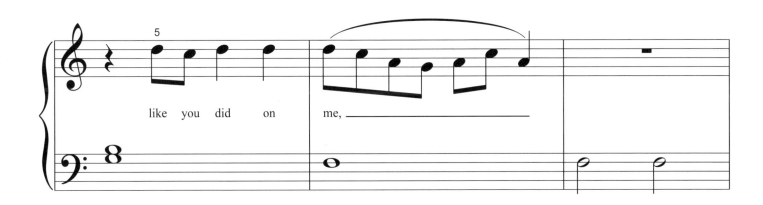

like you did on

me, _____

like you did on

me. _____

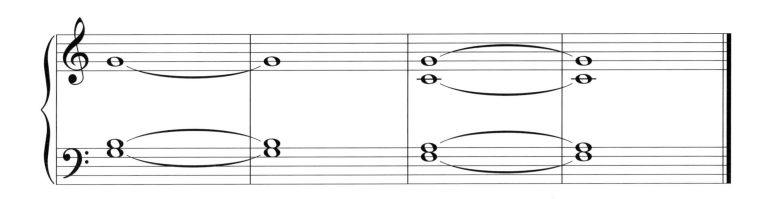

NEVER BREAK

Words and Music by JOHN STEPHENS, GREG WELLS,
NASRI ATWEH and BENJAMIN MCILDOWIE

Moderately

We got a good thing, babe.
More than a good sen - sa - tion;

When - ev - er life is hard,
more than a pass - ing fling.

we'll nev - er lose our way, 'cause we both
You are the ex - pla - na - tion of what

know who we are. ____
love real - ly means. ____

Who knows a - bout to - mor - row? We don't
Big - ger than you and me, it's "one plus

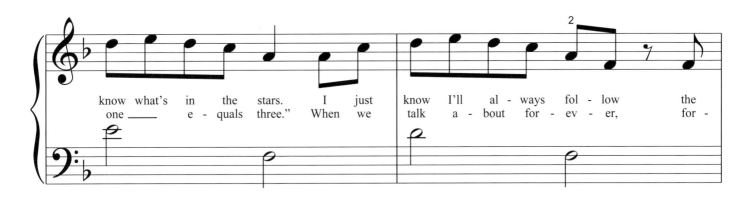

know what's in the stars. I just know I'll al - ways fol - low the
one ___ e - quals three." When we talk a - bout for - ev - er, for -

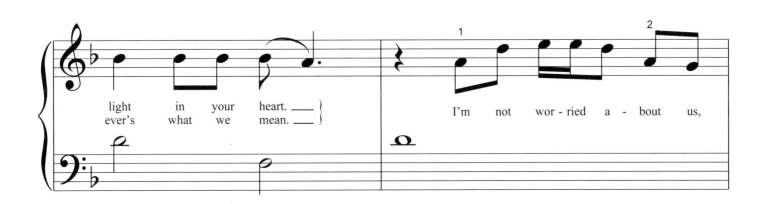

light in your heart. ___ I'm not wor - ried a - bout us,
ever's what we mean. ___

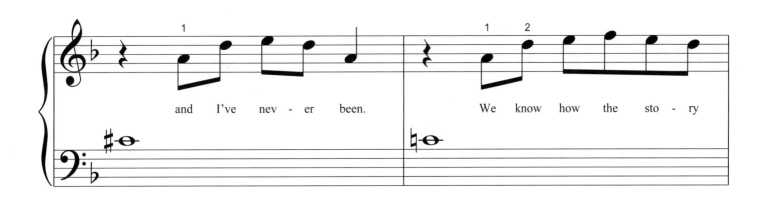

and I've nev - er been. We know how the sto - ry

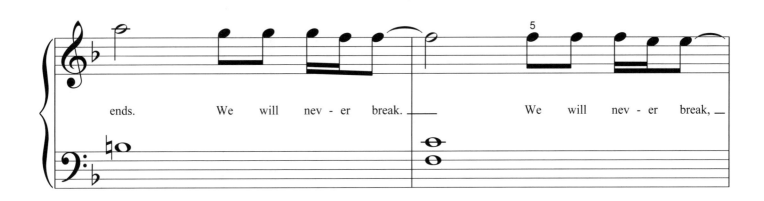

ends. We will nev - er break. ___ We will nev - er break, ___

_____ built on a foun - da - tion strong e - nough to stay. We will nev - er

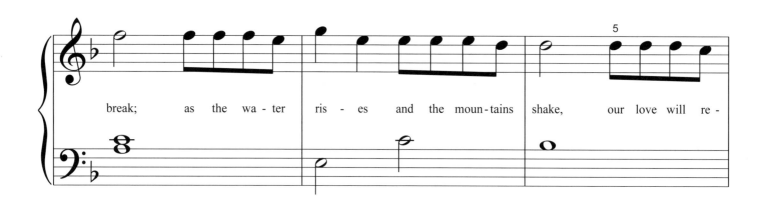

break; as the wa - ter ris - es and the moun-tains shake, our love will re -

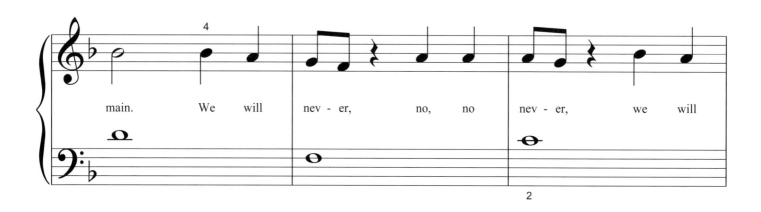

main. We will nev - er, no, no nev - er, we will

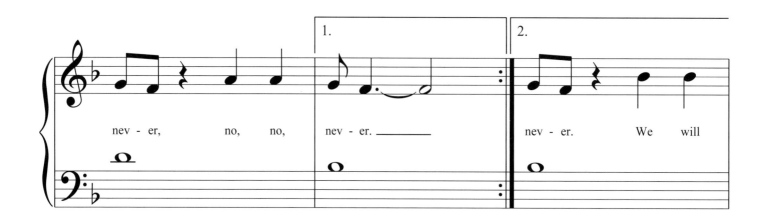

nev - er, no, no, nev - er. _____ nev - er. We will

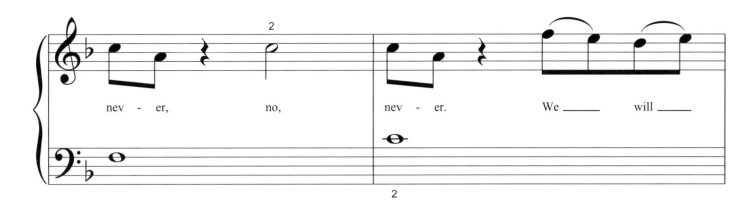

nev - er,   no,   nev - er.   We _____ will _____

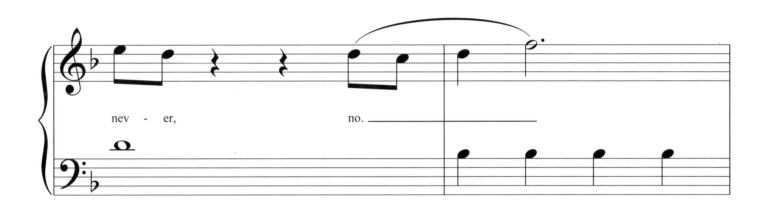

nev - er,   no. _____

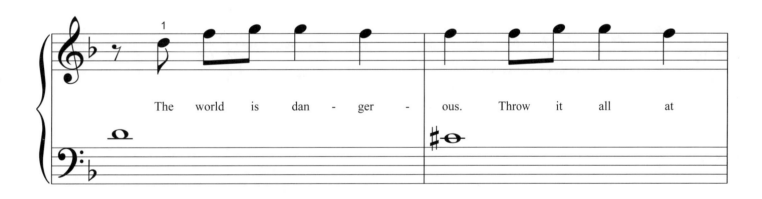

The world is dan - ger - ous. Throw it all at

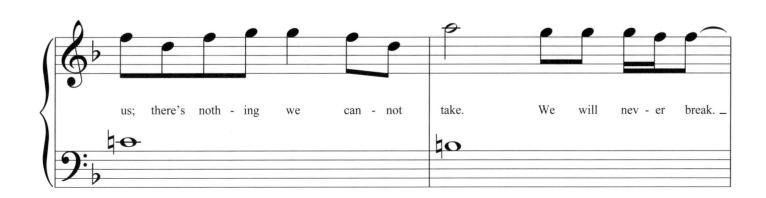

us; there's noth - ing we can - not take.   We will nev - er break. _

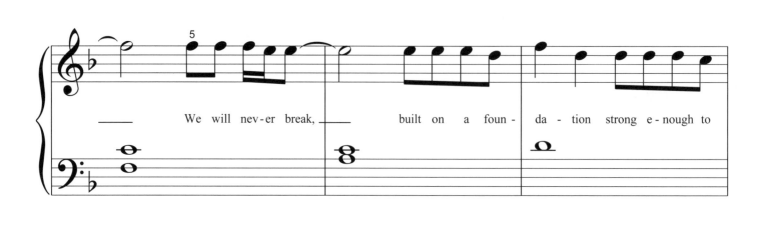

We will nev-er break, _____ built on a foun - da - tion strong e - nough to

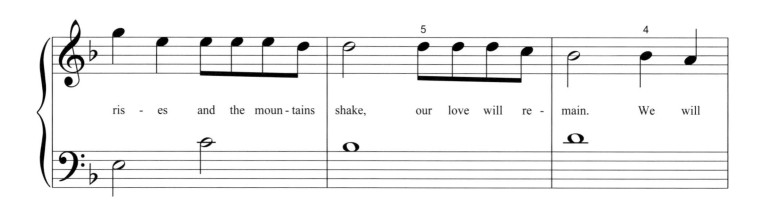

stay. We will nev - er break; as the wa - ter

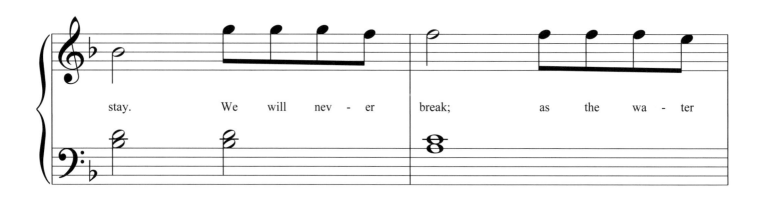

ris - es and the moun - tains shake, our love will re - main. We will

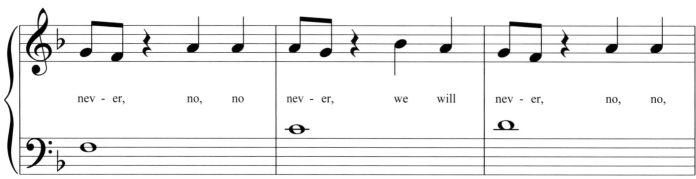

nev - er, no, no nev - er, we will nev - er, no, no,

2

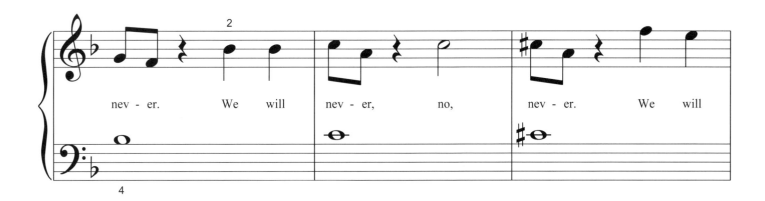

nev - er.   We   will   nev - er,   no,   nev - er.   We   will

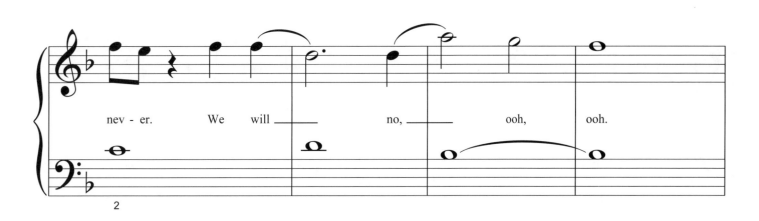

nev - er,   no. _____ We   will   nev - er,   no,

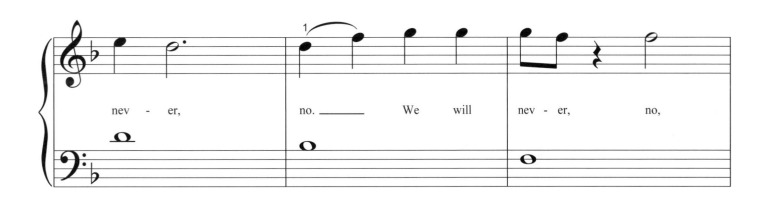

nev - er.   We   will _____ no, _____ ooh,   ooh.

SOMEONE YOU LOVED

Words and Music by LEWIS CAPALDI,
BENJAMIN KOHN, PETER KELLEHER,
THOMAS BARNES and SAMUEL ROMAN

Moderate Ballad

I'm go-ing un-der, and this time I fear there's no one to
I'm go-ing un-der, and this time I fear there's no one to

save me.
turn to.

This "all or noth-ing" real-ly
This "all or noth-ing" way of

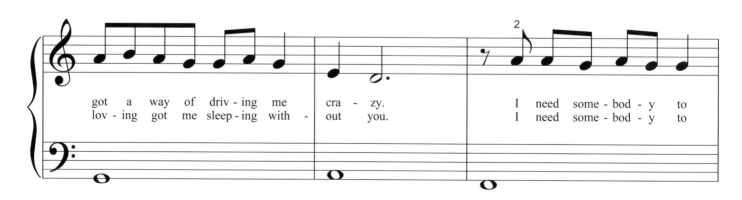

got a way of driv-ing me cra-zy.
lov-ing got me sleep-ing with-out you.

I need some-bod-y to
I need some-bod-y to

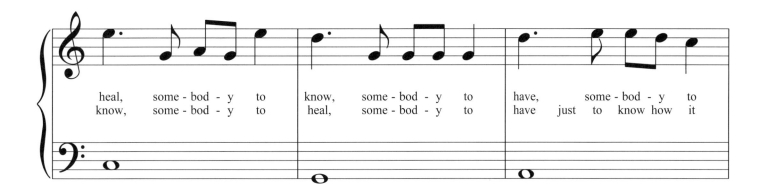

heal, some-bod-y to know, some-bod-y to have, some-bod-y to
know, some-bod-y to heal, some-bod-y to have just to know how it

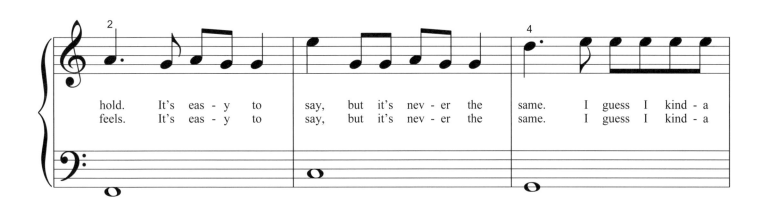

hold. It's eas-y to say, but it's nev-er the same. I guess I kind-a
feels. It's eas-y to say, but it's nev-er the same. I guess I kind-a

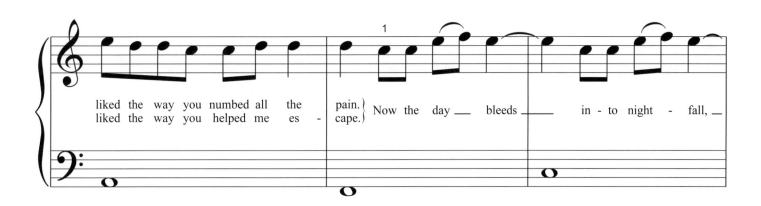

liked the way you numbed all the pain. } Now the day __ bleeds ___ in-to night - fall, __
liked the way you helped me es - cape. }

__ and you're not here to get me through it all. I let my guard down,

and then you pulled the rug. ____ I was get - ting kind - a used to be - ing some-one you

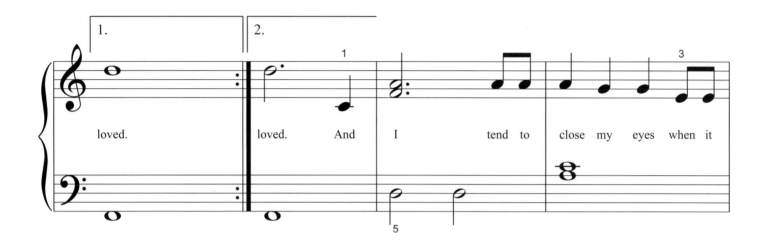

1.
loved.

2.
loved. And I tend to close my eyes when it

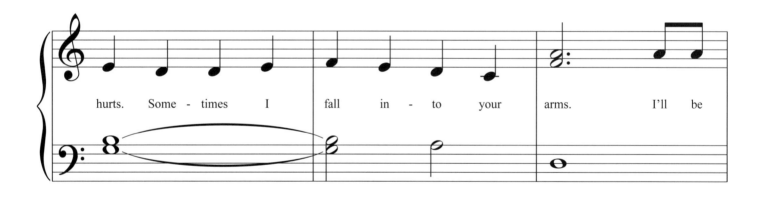

hurts. Some - times I fall in - to your arms. I'll be

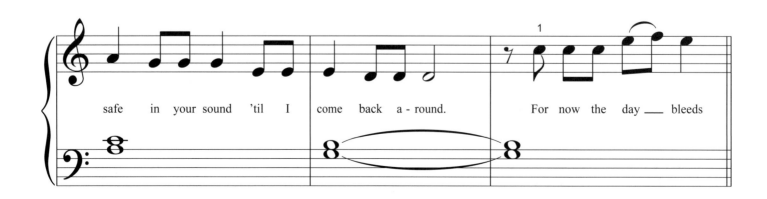

safe in your sound 'til I come back a - round. For now the day ___ bleeds

in - to night - fall, ____ and you're not here to get me through it all.

I let my guard down, and then you pulled the rug. ____ I was get - ting kind - a

used to be - ing some - one you loved. {But now the day bleeds / I let my guard down and then you pulled the rug. _

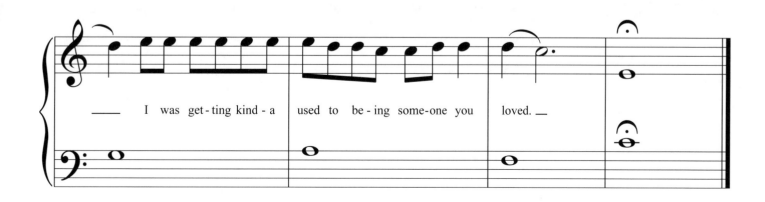

_ I was get - ting kind - a used to be - ing some-one you loved. _

WONDER

Words and Music by SHAWN MENDES, THOMAS HULL,
SCOTT HARRIS and NATE MERCEREAU

Moderately

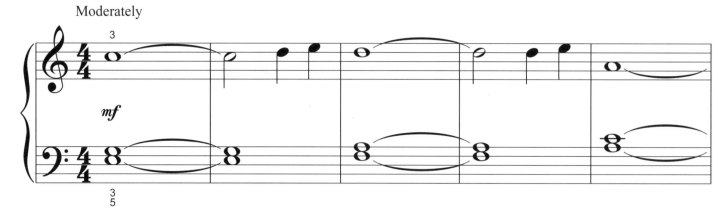

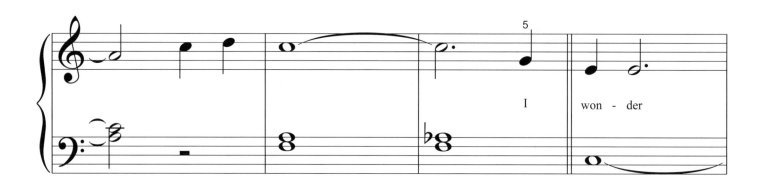

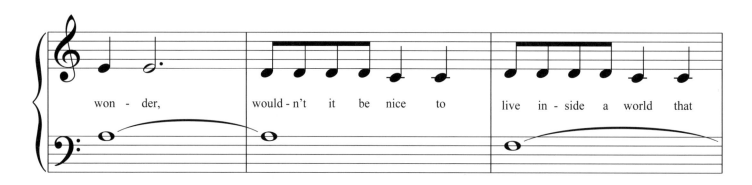

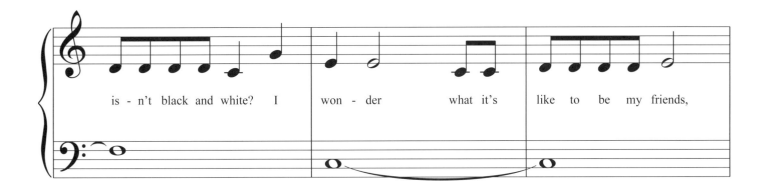

is - n't black and white? I wonder what it's like to be my friends,

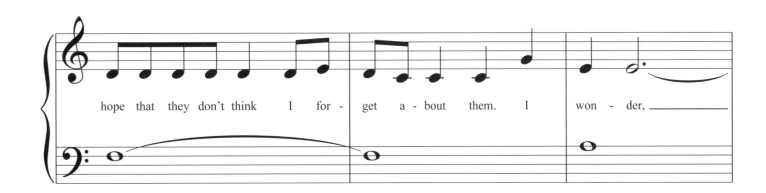

hope that they don't think I for - get a - bout them. I wonder, ____

____ I wonder. ____ Right be - fore I

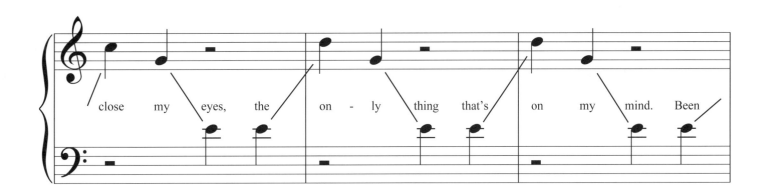

close my eyes, the on - ly thing that's on my mind. Been

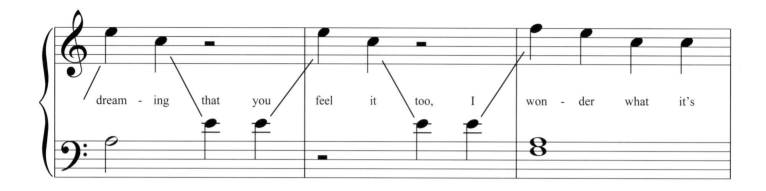

dream - ing　that　you　feel　it　too,　I　won - der　what　it's

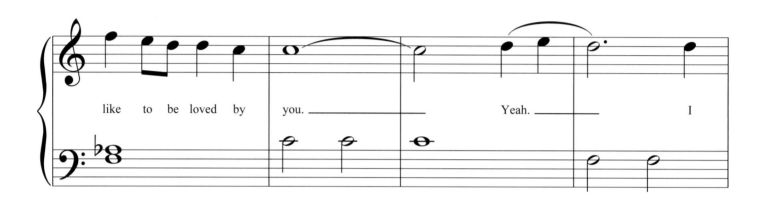

like　to　be　loved　by　you. _____　Yeah. _____　I

won - der　what　it's　like. _____　I　won - der　what　it's

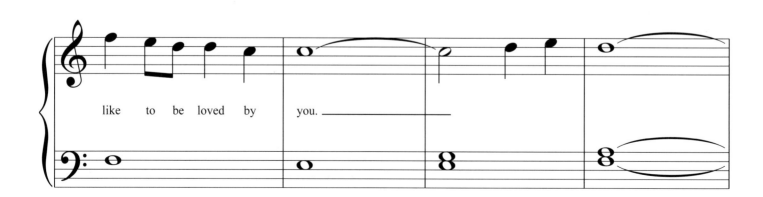

like　to　be　loved　by　you. _____

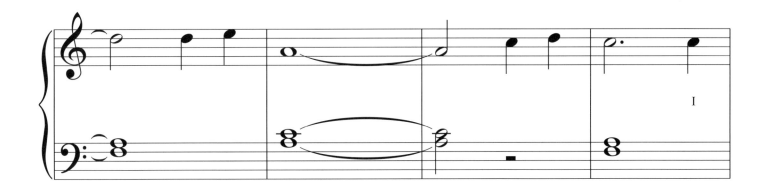

YOU SAY

Words and Music by LAUREN DAIGLE,
JASON INGRAM and PAUL MABURY

Moderately

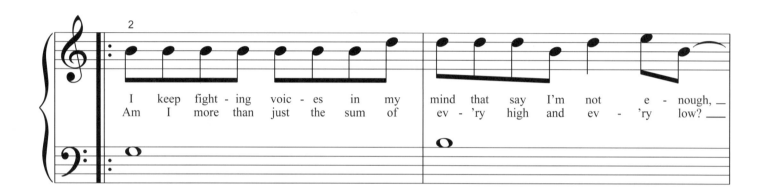

I keep fight-ing voic-es in my mind that say I'm not e-nough, __
Am I more than just the sum of ev-'ry high and ev-'ry low? __

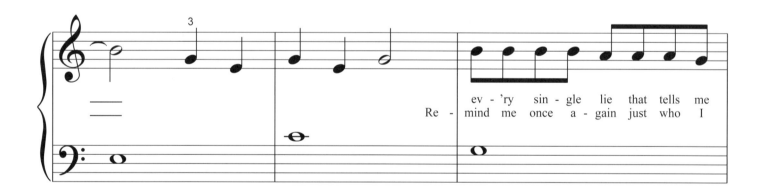

ev-'ry sin-gle lie that tells me
Re-mind me once a-gain just who I

I will nev-er meas-ure up.
am, be-cause I need to know.

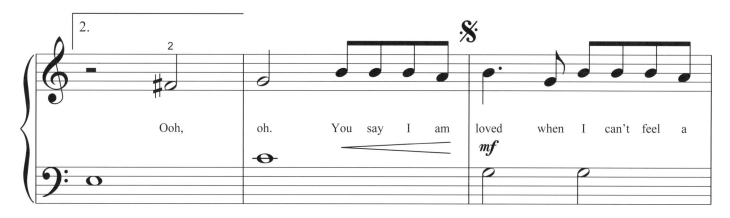

Ooh, oh. You say I am loved when I can't feel a

mf

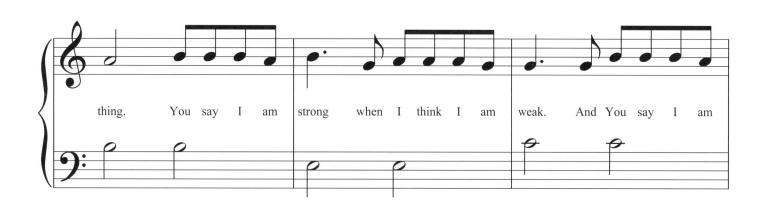

thing. You say I am strong when I think I am weak. And You say I am

held when I am fall - ing short. And when I don't be - long, oh, You say I am

Yours, and I be - lieve, oh, I be - lieve what You say of

45

To Coda

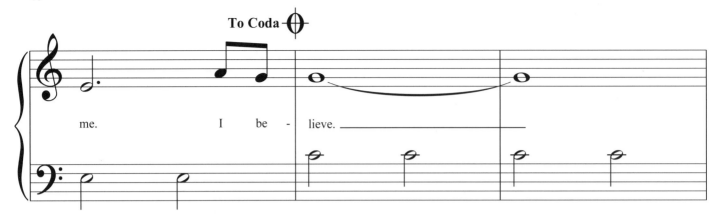

me.   I   be -   lieve. _____

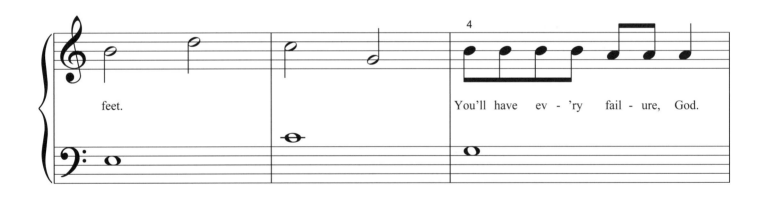

Tak - ing all I have, and now I'm   lay - ing it at Your

feet.   You'll have ev - 'ry fail - ure, God.

D.S. al Coda

You'll have ev - 'ry vic - to - ry.   Ooh,   oh.   You say I am

CODA

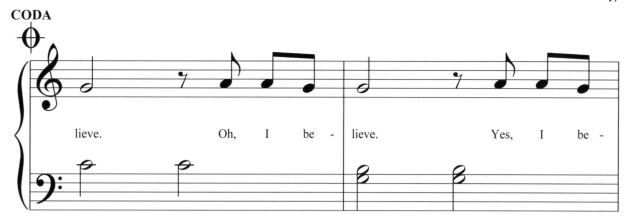

lieve. Oh, I be - lieve. Yes, I be -

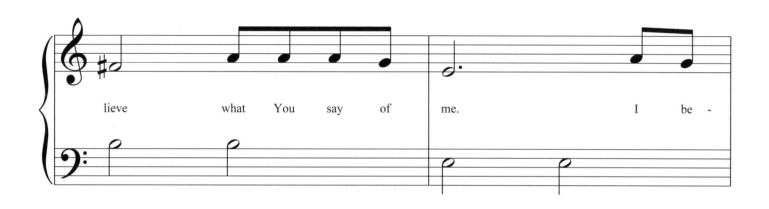

lieve what You say of me. I be -

lieve.

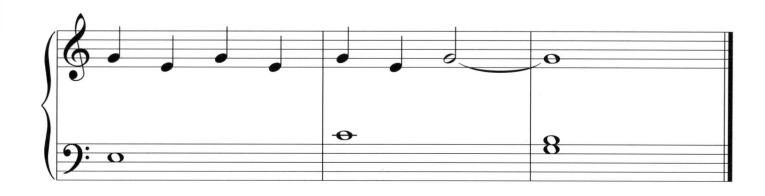

BEGINNING PIANO SOLO

Hal Leonard Beginning Piano Solos are created for students in the first and second years of study. These arrangements include a simple presentation of melody and harmony for a first "solo" experience. Go to **halleonard.com** for song lists.

Adele
00156395 10 songs $15.99

The Beatles
00306568 8 songs $14.99

Songs of the Beatles
00307153 8 songs $10.99

Beethoven
00338054 10 songs $9.99

Broadway Favorites
00319408 10 songs $9.99

Cartoon Favorites
00279152 10 songs $9.99

A Charlie Brown Christmas
00311767 10 songs $12.99

Charlie Brown Favorites
00153652 12 songs $10.99

Chart Hits
00362594 10 songs $12.99

Christmastime
00101873 8 songs $9.99

Classical Favorites
00311063 8 songs $8.99

Contemporary Disney Solos
00316082 10 songs $14.99

Disney Classics
00311431 9 songs $10.99

Disney Favorites
00334221 10 songs $12.99

Disney Hits
00264691 10 songs $10.99

Billie Eilish
00362598 10 songs $14.99

First Book of Disney Solos
00316058 8 songs $12.99

Frozen
00130375 7 songs $14.99

Frozen 2
00329567 8 songs $14.99

Gospel Hymn Favorites
00311799 10 songs $9.99

Great TV Themes
00319409 10 songs $9.99

Greatest Pop Hits
00311064 8 songs $9.95

Happy Songs
00346762 10 songs $10.99

Hit Movie Songs
00338186 10 songs $9.99

It's a Beautiful Day with Mister Rogers
00319418 7 songs $8.99

Jazz Standards
00311065 8 songs $9.95

Best of Carole King
00118420 8 songs $10.99

Les Misérables
00103351 9 songs $14.99

The Lion King
00319465 9 songs $12.99

The Most Beautiful Songs Ever
00110402 50 songs $14.99

The Phantom of the Opera
00103239 9 songs $14.99

Pop Hits
00175142 10 songs $10.99

Praise & Worship Favorites
00311271 8 songs $9.95

The Sound of Music
00316037 10 songs $10.99

Star Wars
00110287 10 songs $14.99

Best of Taylor Swift
00175650 10 songs $12.99

10 Fun Favorites
00110390 10 songs $9.99

Top Hits of 2016
00194558 10 songs $9.99

Wicked
00109365 8 songs $14.99

John Williams
00194545 14 songs $11.99

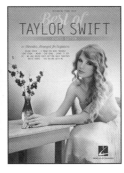
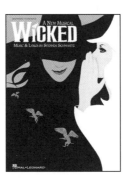

HAL•LEONARD®

Order these and many more songbooks from your favorite music retailer at
halleonard.com